Bond

Maths

Assessment Papers

8–9 years

J M Bond
Andrew Baines

OXFORD
UNIVERSITY PRESS

Great Clarendon Street, Oxford, OX2 6DP, United Kingdom

Oxford University Press is a department of the University of Oxford. It furthers the University's objective of excellence in research, scholarship, and education by publishing worldwide. Oxford is a registered trade mark of Oxford University Press in the UK and in certain other countries

First published in 2001 by Nelson Thornes Ltd
This edition published in 2014

British Library Cataloguing in Publication Data
Data available

978-1-4085-2514-2

10 9 8 7 6 5 4 3 2 1

Printed in China

Acknowledgements

Page make-up: OKS Prepress, India
Illustrations: Tech-Set Limited

Before you get started

What is Bond?

This book is part of the Bond Assessment Papers series for maths, which provides **thorough and continuous practice of all the key maths content** from ages five to thirteen. Bond's maths resources are ideal preparation for many different kinds of tests and exams – from SATs to 11+ and other secondary school selection exams.

What does this book cover?

It covers all the maths that a child of this age would be expected to learn and is fully in line with the National Curriculum for maths and the National Numeracy Strategy. One of the key features of Bond Assessment Papers is that each one practises **a wide variety of skills and question types** so that children are always challenged to think – and don't get bored repeating the same question type again and again. We think that variety is the key to effective learning. It helps children 'think on their feet' and cope with the unexpected.

The age given on the cover is for guidance only. As the papers are designed to be reasonably challenging for the age group, any one child may naturally find him or herself working above or below the stated age. The important thing is that children are always encouraged by their performance. Working at the right level is the key to this.

What does the book contain?

- **24 papers** – each one contains 40 questions.
- **Scoring devices** – there are score boxes in the margins and a Progress Chart on page 64. The chart is a visual and motivating way for children to see how they are doing. Encouraging them to colour in the chart as they go along and to try to beat their last score can be highly effective!
- **Next Steps** – advice on what to do after finishing the papers can be found on the inside back cover.
- **Answers** – located in an easily-removed central pull-out section.
- **Key maths words** – on page 1 you will find a glossary of special key words that are used in the papers. These are highlighted in bold each time that they appear. These words are now used in the maths curriculum and children are expected to know them at this age.

How can you use this book?

One of the great strengths of Bond Assessment Papers is their flexibility. They can be used at home, school and by tutors to:

- provide regular maths practice in **bite-sized chunks**
- **highlight strengths and weaknesses** in the core skills

- identify **individual needs**
- set **homework**
- set **timed formal practice** tests – allow about 30 minutes.

It is best to start at the beginning and work though the papers in order.

What does a score mean and how can it be improved?

If children colour in the Progress Chart at the back, this will give you an idea of how they are doing. The Next Steps inside the back cover will help you to decide what to do next to help a child progress. We suggest that it is always valuable to go over any wrong answers with children.

Don't forget the website …!

Visit www.bond11plus.co.uk for lots of advice, information and suggestions on everything to do with Bond, exams, and helping children to do their best.

Key words

Some special maths words are used in this book. You will find them in **bold** each time they appear in the papers. These words are explained here.

area the space inside a shape. Area is measured in square units, for example square centimetres (cm^2) or square metres (m^2)

cube a solid shape whose faces are all squares, such as a child's building block

cuboid a solid shape whose faces are either all rectangles, or rectangles and squares such as a cereal packet

digit any single number, for example 4 has one digit, 37 has two digits, 437 has three digits

divisible can be divided by, for example 4 is divisible by 2

equilateral triangle a triangle which has all its sides of the same length

faces flat sides of a solid object

heptagon a shape with seven sides

hexagon a shape with six sides

isosceles triangle a triangle which has two sides the same length

mirror line the line in which a shape can be reflected, like the reflection in a mirror

multiple a number which another number multiplies into, for example 3, 6, 9, 12, 15, 60, 93 are multiples of 3

net the flat shape that a three-dimensional object, such as a box, will make if you open it out

octagon a shape with 8 sides

parallelogram a four-sided shape that has its opposite sides parallel

pentagon a shape with five sides

perimeter the distance round the outside of a shape

pictogram a diagram that records something using pictures

polygon a shape with three or more sides

product the answer when you multiply two numbers together, for example the product of 4 and 2 is 8

quadrilateral a shape with 4 sides

round means roughly or approximately, for example 42 rounded to the nearest 10 is 40, 470 rounded to the nearest 100 is 500

semicircle a shape which is half a circle

square a square is a rectangle with four equal sides

sum the answer when you add two numbers together. The sum of 2 and 4 is 6

symmetry if a shape has symmetry it has one or more mirror lines like this:

tetrahedron a solid shape with four triangular faces

Venn diagram a chart for sorting information of different kinds

Paper 1

The area of this square ☐ = 1, what is the area of each of the shapes below?

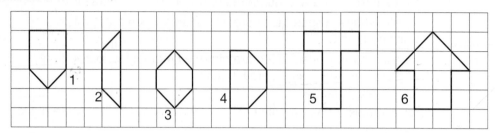

1 __5__

2 __3__

3 __4½__

4 __4 5__

5 __4 6__

6 __8__

7 Rachel is twice as old as Amy. If Amy is 7, how old is Rachel?

__14__

○ 1

8 How many faces does this **cube** have?   __6__

9 Underline the correct answer. Each face on the **cube** is:

    a triangle   <u>a square</u>   a circle   a rectangle

10 How many **faces** does this **cuboid** have?   __6__

11 Underline the correct answer. Each face on the **cuboid** is:

    a triangle   a square   a circle   <u>a rectangle</u>

○ 4

There are 60 minutes in an hour. How many minutes are there between:

12   06:19   and   06:30   11

13   02:27   and   02:50   33

14   05:50   and   06:10   20

15   07:51   and   08:00   9

16   12:01   and   12:40   39

17   04:52   and   05:10   70   ◯ 6

Underline the correct answer on each line.

18	$100 - 29 =$	**81**	79	71	89	129
19	$56 \div 7 =$	8	9	7	**6**	10
20	$47 + 35 =$	72	73	81	71	**82**
21	$\frac{1}{2} + \frac{1}{2} =$	$\frac{1}{4}$	$\frac{1}{2}$	**1**	2	4

◯ 4

22–23 Fill in the missing numbers on this number line.

−2   −1   0   1   2   3   4

24–25 Fill in the missing numbers on this number line.

−5   −4   −3   −2   −1   0   1

26–29 Fill in the missing numbers on this number line.

−7   −6   −5   −4   −3   −2   −1   ◯ 8

Maria was born 5 July 2004.   Anita was born 19 April 2004.

Daley was born 31 October 2004.   David was born 8 November 2003.

30–31   david   is the eldest and   daley   is the youngest.

32–34 On 5 July 2006 Maria was ___born___ , Anita was ___11___
and ___Jason___ was 12.

35–37 ___× 6___

12	72
20	600
40	240

600 120

38–40 ___+ 5___

60	300
80	400
90	450

Now go to the Progress Chart to record your score!   Total

Paper 2

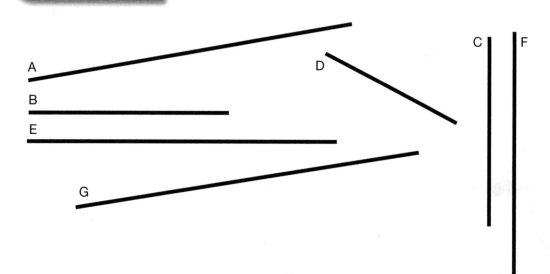

Measure each line and answer the questions.

1 The longest sloping line is ___G___ .

2 The longest vertical line is ___F___ .

3 The longest horizontal line is ___E___ .

4 What is the difference in length between the two horizontal lines?
___$3\frac{1}{2}$___ cm

5 What is the difference in length between the two vertical lines?
___$1\frac{1}{2}$___ cm

6 The two vertical lines added together are ___$11\frac{1}{2}$___ cm long.

7 The two horizontal lines added together are ___14___ cm long.

8 What is the **product** of 5 and 7? _12_ ① 1

There are 60 children altogether in Class 2 and Class 3.

    9 If there are 32 in Class 2, how many are in Class 3? _38_

George has three times as much money as Michael.

    10 Michael has 14p, so how much has George? _48p_ ② 2

        312   123   321

11 In which number is the figure 1 a unit? _321_

12 In which number is the figure 1 a ten? _312_

13 In which number is the figure 1 a hundred? _123_ ③ 3

14 What number needs to go in the box? Write it in.

    4732 = [4000] + 700 + 30 + 2

15 What number needs to go in the box? Write it in.

    5935 = 5000 + [900] + 30 + 5

16 What number needs to go in the box? Write it in.

    3941 = 3000 + 900 + [40] + 1

17 What number needs to go in the box? Write it in.

    5864 = 5000 + 800 + 60 + [4]

18 What number needs to go in the box? Write it in.

    9573 = [9000] + 500 + 70 + 3

19 What number needs to go in the box? Write it in.

    1633 = 1000 + [600] + 30 + 3

20 What number needs to go in the box? Write it in.

    7488 = 7000 + 400 + [80] + 8 ⑦ 7

21–22 Fill in the missing numbers on this number line.

13	15	17	19	_21_	23	25	_27_

2

Underline the correct answer in each line.

23 £1 − 11p	=	1p	<u>89p</u>	£1.11	99p	£1.01
24 8p + 6p + 7p	=	20p	22p	19p	<u>21p</u>	23p
25 66 + 26	=	<u>92</u>	87	82	83	93
26 105 ÷ 3	=	15	33	<u>35</u>	41	51
27 $\frac{1}{2}$ of 40	=	80	10	2	40	<u>20</u>
28 1000 ÷ 10	=	500	10	20	100	<u>1000</u>

6

Mum, Dad, Helen and Andrew went to the zoo.

Chartwell Zoo

Entrance: Adults £22.50
Children £15.50
Monkey House: £5.00
Ice Cream: £4 £1.60

29 How much did it cost for all of them to go in? _£76_

30 How much did it cost for all of them to go in the monkey house?
_£20_

31 How much did it cost them to have an ice cream each? _~~£6.40~~_

32 How much did they spend at the zoo altogether? _£102.40_

4

There were 35 children in a class.

33–34 If the number of boys was one more than the number of girls, there
are _18_ boys and _17_ girls.

2

6

Here is part of a ruler.

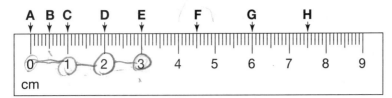

cm

35 How far is it from A to G? _____6cm_____

36 How far is it from B to E? _____$2\frac{1}{2}$cm_____

37 How far is it from D to H? _____$5\frac{1}{2}$cm_____

38 How far is it from C to F? _____$3\frac{1}{2}$cm_____ (4)

39 What number, when divided by 9 gives an answer of 6? _____54_____

40 How many times will 10 go into 200? _____20_____ (2)

Now go to the Progress Chart to record your score! Total (40)

Paper 3

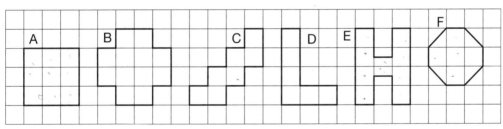

1 The area of shape A is __9__ squares.

2 The area of shape B is __12__ squares.

3 The area of shape C is __7__ squares.

4 The area of shape D is __6__ squares.

5 The area of shape E is __9__ squares.

6 The area of shape F is __7__ squares. (6)

7 In every 2 weeks I spend 10 days at school. So in every 5 weeks
  I spend __25__ days at school.

8 In every 3 days I spend 4 hours reading. So in every _15_ days I spend 20 hours reading.

9 With every box of cereal you get 4 tokens, and the toy you want requires 24 tokens.

How many boxes of cereal do you have to buy? _6_

10 In every *Kid's App* magazine you get 3 transfers. In 3 *Kid's App* magazines you get _9_ transfers.

11–15 Underline the numbers which can be divided exactly by 5.

52   <u>25</u>   <u>40</u>   24   <u>45</u>   54   <u>60</u>   51   <u>15</u>

16 Write in words 7001. _seven thousand and one_

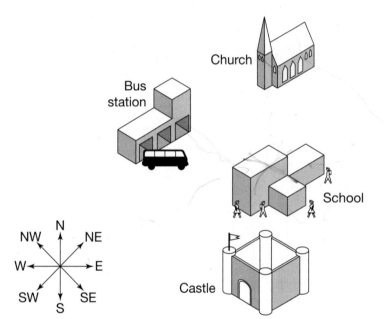

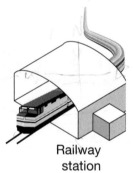

In which direction is:

17 the school from the railway station?

18 the castle from the school?

19 the bus station from the school?

20 the church from the bus station?

21 the railway station from church?

22 the castle from the church?

23 the school from the bus station?

W
S
NW
NE
SE
S
SE

What number is halfway between:

24 50 and 70? _60_

25 35 and 55? _25_

26 25 and 35? _30_

27 12 and 20? _____ ○ 4

28 Jane was born in 2008. Jock is 3 years older than Jane. In what year was he born? _2005_

29 Leanne was born in 2005. In what year was she 6? _2011_

30 Rehman was 12 in 2011. In what year was she born? _1999_ ○ 3

31–33 Reflect these shapes in the **mirror line**.

○ 3

34 What is the biggest number you can make with these **digits**: 3, 6, 4, 8? _8,643_

35 Now write it in words. _eight thousand six hundred and fortythree_

36 What is the biggest number you can make with these **digits**: 2, 3, 4, 0? _4,230_

37 Now write it in words. _four thousand two hundred and thirty_

38 Write in figures three thousand, two hundred and fifty-four. _3,254_ ○ 5

39 What is one quarter of 60? _15_

40 How many minutes are there between 10:45 and 11:10? _25 mins_ ○ 2

Paper 4

1   73
    35
+ 98
206

2   58
× 6
38

3   £6.98
+ £0.42
_____

   3

4–9 Fill in the missing numbers to balance the scales.

21 + 3	△	6 ×
5 ×	△	28 + 7
70 − 10	△	5 ×
45 −	△	6 × 7
6 × 9	△	60 −
17 +	△	50 − 10

6

Our class
Cats and dogs

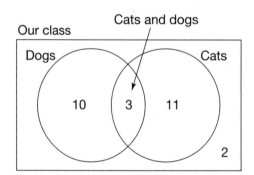

Dogs   10   3   11   Cats

2

Our class made this **Venn diagram** to show how many of us have cats and dogs.

10 How many children have dogs?   _____

11 How many have cats?   _____

12 How many have both a cat and a dog?   _____

13 How many children haven't got a dog?   _____

14 How many children haven't got a cat?   _____

15 How many children are there in the class?   _____

6

16 When a number was added to 16 the answer was 25.
What was the number? ________ 1

17 What temperature does this thermometer show? ________

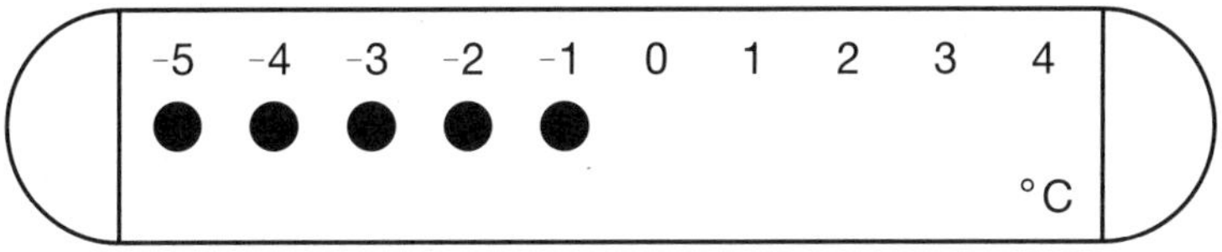

18 Draw a circle around the lowest temperature: -7 °C, -9 °C 2

19 Kay was 9 in 2010. In what year was she born? ________

20 Martin was born in December 2007 and Michael was born in January 2008.

Who is the elder? ________ 2

This **pictogram** shows the number of children in our school.

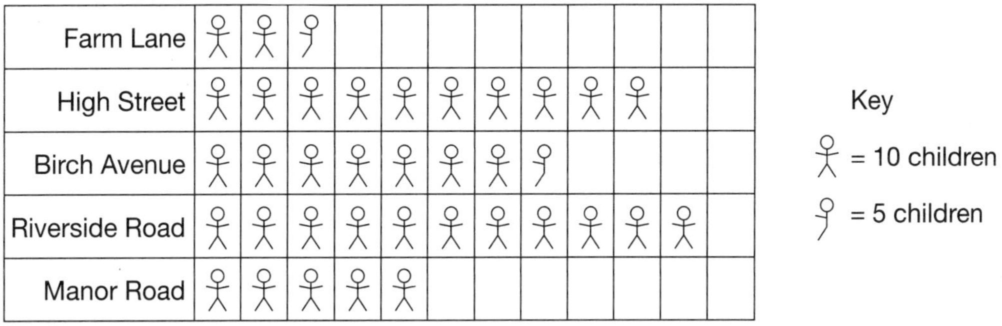

21 How many children are there in the school? ________

22 In which road or street do most children live? ________

23 Twice as many children live in the High Street as in ________

24 There are three times as many children in Birch Avenue as in

________.

25–28 Twenty more children come to our school. Five live in Farm Lane, 5 in Riverside Road and 10 in Birch Avenue. Show this on the **pictogram**.

29 How many will there now be in our school? ________ 9

30 How much greater is 33 than 19? _____

31 I spent 77p and had 15p left. How much did I have at first? _____

32 What is the cost of 3 packets of crisps at 26p each? _____

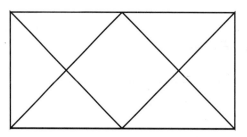

Look closely at the shape above.

33 How many **squares** does it contain? _____

34 How many rectangles does it contain? _____

35 How many triangles does it contain? _____

One question on each line has a different answer from the others.

Draw a line under it.

| **36** | 5 × 10 | 45 + 5 | 10 × 5 | 60 − 5 | 47 + 3 |
| **37** | 7 × 6 | 4 × 12 | 6 × 8 | 42 + 6 | 50 − 2 |

38 What number is 1 less than 300? _____

39 The number which is 2 more than 278 is _____

40 If I took 10 from 106 it would leave _____

Paper 5

1 Draw a circle around the highest temperature: −8 °C,   −9 °C

2–3 Fill in the missing numbers on this number line.

_____   −1   0   1   2   _____   4

Underline the correct answer in each line.

4 11×11 = 110 111 121 132 122

5 $150 \div 30$ = 50 5 30 20 55

6 $70 - 39$ = 41 49 39 109 31

7 $1\frac{1}{2}$ hours = 75 min 90 min 45 min 85 min 15 min

8 1.5 kg = 150 g 505 g 1500 g 1050 g 105 g

9 $510 \div 5$ = 21 102 120 12 121

10 150 cm = 15 m 0.15 m 150 m 50 m 1.5 m

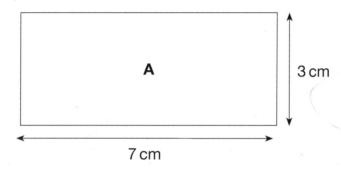

A

3 cm

7 cm

11 What is the **area** of rectangle A? _____ cm^2

12 What is the **perimeter** of rectangle A? _____ cm

B

3 cm

17 cm

13 What is the **area** of rectangle B? _____ cm^2

14 What is the **perimeter** of rectangle B? _____ cm

Fill in the missing number in each question.

15 $3 + 4 +$ _____ = 10

16 $5 + 1 -$ _____ = 4

17 $3 + 3 +$ _____ = 9

18–22 Underline the numbers which are **divisible** by 7.

19   49   28   56   62   35   77   79

5

23–26 Underline the numbers which are **multiples** of 6.

36   72   26   96   56   24   28

4

Here is part of a centimetre ruler.

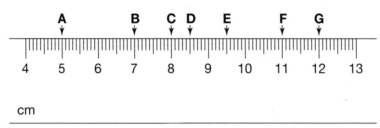

cm

27 How far is it from A to B? _____

28 How far is it from C to D? _____

29 How far is it from A to D? _____

30 How far is it from B to F? _____

31 How far is it from C to G? _____

32 How far is it from E to G? _____

6

Write the next two numbers in each line.

33–34   6   12   18   24   30   ____   ____

35–36   50   47   44   41   38   ____   ____

4

Underline the larger of each pair.

37 (6 × 10)   or   (3 × 22)

38 (5 × 20)   or   (11 × 10)

39 (10 × 10) or   (3 × 30)

40 (3 × 50)   or   (4 × 40)

4

Now go to the Progress Chart to record your score!   Total   40

Paper 6

1
```
   37
+ 46
─────
```

2
```
   72
-  39
─────
```

3
```
   36
×   3
─────
```

4
```
    ─────
2) 108
```

5–10 Complete the following bus timetable. Each bus takes the same amount of time to do the journey.

Bus	A	B	C
High Street	2:40	3:50	
Broad Lane		4:00	5:05
Market Place	2:55		
Kent Road	3:05		

Two shelves are 65 cm and 89 cm long.

11 What is their total length in metres? _____

12 What is the difference in their lengths in centimetres? _____

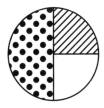

13 What fraction of the circle is spotted? _____

14 What fraction is striped? _____

15 What fraction is plain? _____

16 How many times larger is the spotted part than the striped part? _____

17–23 Complete the empty brackets in this multiplication table.

×	4	5	( )
	( )	10	( )
	12	( )	18
	( )	20	( )
	20	( )	

24 164 × 4 = _____

25 182 × 6 = _____

Put the correct sign in the spaces.

26–27 3 _____ 4 = 6 _____ 1

28–29 5 _____ 4 = 2 _____ 7

30–31 3 _____ 3 = 8 _____ 1

32–33 8 _____ 1 = 5 _____ 2

This **pictogram** shows how the children in Class 4 come to school.

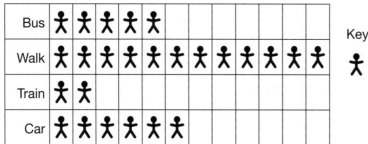

Key

☓ = 1 child

34 How many children are there in the class? _____

35 How many more walk than come by car? _____

36 How many more come by car than by bus? _____

37 How many children don't come by bus? _____

38 How many more children walk than come by bus? _____

39 How many children don't come by train? _____

40 How many times can I take 9 from 54? _____

7

2

8

6

1

Paper 7

1 345 ÷ 5 = _____

2 345 + 456 = _____

3 321 × 3 = _____

4–6 Fill in the missing numbers on this number line.

−7 _____ −5 _____ −3 _____ −1

7 Draw a circle around the highest temperature: −17 °C,   −29 °C

8–12 Put these temperature in order, lowest first.

0 °C,   −4 °C,   −7 °C,   3 °C,   −1 °C _____

13 My watch was 5 minutes fast. It showed 10:30.
What was the right time?   _____ : _____

Afternoon school begins at 1:30 and finishes at 3:35.

14 For how long do we work in the afternoon?   _____ hr _____ min

15 What change should I have from £1.00 if I spent 67p?   _____ p

16–20 Change this recipe for ginger nuts for 6 people to a recipe for 12
people for a party.

6 people	
125 g	flour
30 g	fat
75 g	sugar
30 ml	treacle
1 teaspoon	ground ginger

12 people	
_____ g	flour
_____ g	fat
_____ g	sugar
_____ ml	treacle
_____ teaspoons	ground ginger

Underline the question in each line which does not have the same answer as
the others.

21   4 × 3   6 × 2   12 × 1   4 × 2

3

3

6

1

2

5

22	4×4	8×2	1×16	3×5
23	6×5	9×4	10×3	15×2
24	$20 \div 4$	$25 \div 6$	$10 \div 2$	$15 \div 3$
25	$16 - 7$	$18 \div 2$	3×3	$4 + 6$
26	$36 \div 3$	6×3	$25 - 7$	$7 + 11$

6

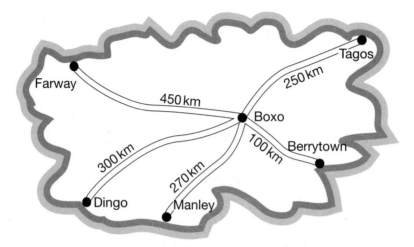

27 Which town is the furthest away from Boxo? _____

28 Which town is the nearest to Boxo? _____

29 How much further is it from Boxo to Farway than it is from Boxo to Manley? _____

3

30–31 Underline the smallest number and circle the largest.

5.7   4.8   7.5   8.4   4.5

2

32 Convert metres into centimetres: 7.45 m = _____ cm

33 **Round** to the nearest pound: £7.49   = £ _____

34 Convert centimetres into metres: 824 cm = _____ m

35 Write 345p in £.   345p   = £ _____

4

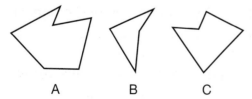
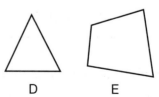

A   B   C   D   E

36–37 Shade in the **quadrilaterals** above.

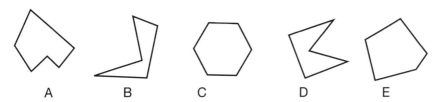

A   B   C   D   E

38–40 Shade in the **pentagons** above.

5

Now go to the Progress Chart to record your score!   Total   40

Paper 8

1 How many pence in £1.25?

2 How many pence in £0.29?

2

A _____

B _____

C _____

D _____

E _____

F _____

3 Line A is _____ cm long.

4 Line B is _____ cm long.

5 Line C is _____ cm long.

6 Line D is _____ cm long.

7 Line E is _____ cm long.

8 Line F is _____ cm long.

9 What is the difference in length between the longest and
the shortest line?   _____ cm

10–11 Lines A and B put together would be the same length as lines _____
and _____ put together.

9

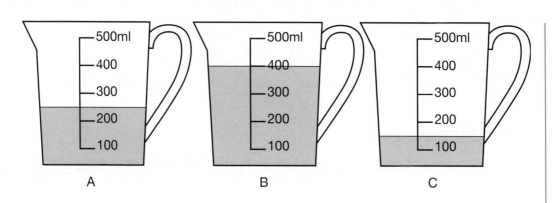

A   B   C

12–14 A has _____ ml.   B has _____ ml.   C has _____ ml.

How many ml of water would you have to add to each jug so that each one holds half a litre?

15–17 A needs _____ ml.   B needs _____ ml.   C needs _____ ml.   ◯ 6

18 What is the remainder when 40 is divided by 6?   _____   ◯ 1

In the number 1234:   how many tens are there?   3

how many hundreds are there?   2

19 In the number 135:   how many tens are there?   _____

20 how many hundreds are there?   _____

21 In the number 1247:   how many units are there?   _____

22 how many hundreds are there?   _____

23 In the number 2439:   how many tens are there?   _____

24 how many thousands are there?   _____   ◯ 6

25 What is $\frac{1}{2}$ of 22?   _____

26 $\frac{1}{3}$ of 24 is   _____

27 $\frac{1}{4}$ of 20 is   _____

28 What is $\frac{1}{5}$ of 15?   _____

29 $\frac{1}{10}$ of 40 is   _____

30 $\frac{1}{3}$ of 27 is   _____   ◯ 6

What are the names of these shapes?

Use the following words to help you:

sphere   triangular prism   **cuboid**   **cube**   cylinder

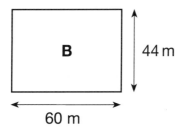

31 _____

32 _____

33 _____

34 _____

35 _____   5

36 John is 120.5 cm tall. James is 4.5 cm shorter.

How tall is James?   _____   1

A	40 cm

60 cm

37 What is the **area** of rectangle A?   _____ cm²

38 What is the **perimeter** of rectangle A?   _____ cm

B	44 m

60 m

39 What is the **area** of rectangle B?   _____ m²

40 What is the **perimeter** of rectangle B?   _____ m   4

Now go to the Progress Chart to record your score!   Total   40

21

Paper 9

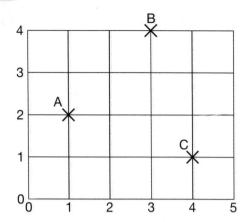

A is 1 square along and 2 squares up from (0,0).

1–2 B is _____ squares along and _____ squares up from (0,0).

3–4 C is _____ squares along and _____ square up from (0,0).

A is at the point (1,2).

5 B is at the point (_____, _____).

6 C is at the point (_____, _____).

7 D is at the point (2,3). Mark it on the grid above.

8 E is at the point (5,0). Mark it on the grid above.

8

9
$$\begin{array}{r} 4.9 \\ + \ 7.5 \\ \hline \\ \hline \end{array}$$

10
$$\begin{array}{r} 3.9 \\ \times \ \ 8 \\ \hline \\ \hline \end{array}$$

2

11 Share 20 cherries among 5 children. They have _____ each.

12 How many glasses holding $\frac{1}{2}$ litre could be filled

from a jug which holds $7\frac{1}{2}$ litres? _____

13 Sally missed the 9:25 a.m. bus. The next one is 17 minutes later.
At what time is the next bus? _____

14 I had 9p after spending 24p. How much did I have at first? _____

15 Aziz walks 4 km each day. In November he walks _____ km.

5

Here is a bar chart which shows the number of hours of sunshine we had each day in the last week of June.

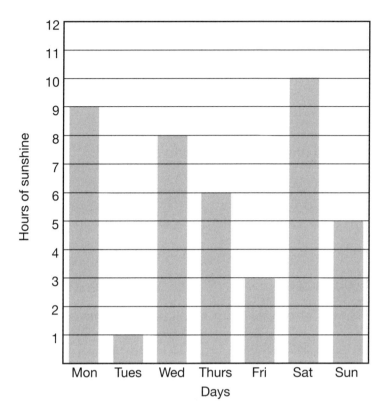

16–17 Which 2 days added together had the same amount of sunshine as Saturday?

_____ and _____

18 It rained on only one day in the week. On which day did it probably rain?

_____

19–21 On which 3 days together did the total sunshine equal that of Monday?

_____ , _____ and _____

22 How many days had fewer than 6 hours of sunshine? _____

23 How many days had more than 8 hours of sunshine? _____

24 What was the total hours of sunshine for the week? _____

25–30 The sunniest day was Saturday. Write the other days in the order of sunniest day to least sunny day.

Saturday, _____ , _____ , _____ ,

_____ , _____ , _____ .

15

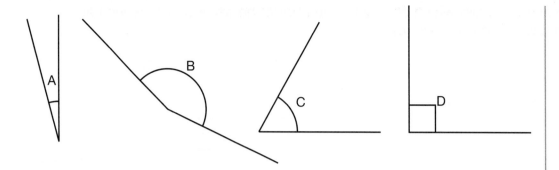

Look at the above angles and answer the following questions.

31 Which angle is the right angle? _____

32 The smallest angle is _____ .

33 The largest angle is _____ .

34 _____ is the 60° angle.

35–38 Place the angles in order of size from smallest to largest.

_____ is less than _____ is less than _____ is less than _____.

8

39 Using the **digits** 5, 6 and 7 make as many 3-figure numbers as you can.

_____ _____ _____ _____ _____ _____

40 Now take away the smallest from the largest. _____

2

Paper 10

1 Write the correct number in the box.

231   ⟶   [   ]
     75 less is

2 Write the correct number in the box.

[   ]   ⟶   260
  62 less is

2

3 Put these numbers in order, smallest to largest.

| 7536 | 6537 | 5736 | 6573 |

_____   _____   _____   _____

Look at this grid.

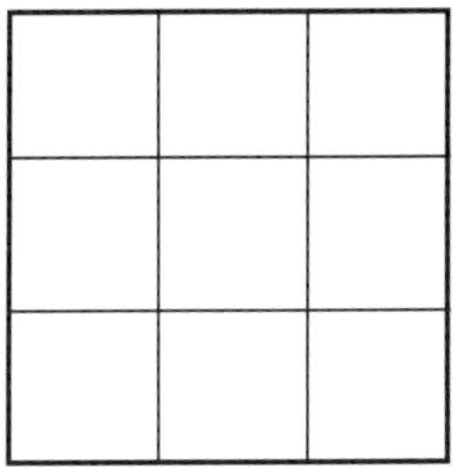

4 How many **squares** of this size are in the grid?

_____

5 How many **squares** of this size are in the grid?

_____

6 How many **squares** of this size are in the grid?

_____

7 What is the total number of **squares** in the grid?

_____

8 What is the smallest number you can make with these **digits**: 3, 5, 4, 9?

_____

9 Now write it in words.

_____

10 What is the largest number you can make with these **digits**: 3, 5, 4, 9?

_____

11 Now write it in words.

_____

12 What is the smallest number you can make with these **digits**: 9, 5, 8, 6, 1?

_____

13 Now write it in words.

_____

14 What is the largest number you can make with these **digits**:
9, 5, 8, 6, 1? _____

15 Now write it in words.

_____

16 Write in figures one thousand, four hundred and eighty-nine.

_____

17 Write in figures seven thousand and eighty-nine. _____ ⬤ 10

Here is a **pictogram** which shows what kind of books are liked most by children in Readwell School.

Key ☺ = 10 children

Mysteries	☺	☺	☺	☺	☺	☺	☺	☺
Travel	☺	☺	☺	☺				
School Stories	☺	☺	☺	☺	☺	☺	☺	☺ ☺
Books on Hobbies	☺	☺	☺					
Animal Stories	☺	☺	☺	☺	☺	☺	☺	

18 Which type of book is most popular? _____

19 Which type of book is least popular? _____

20 How many children are in the school? _____

21 Which kind of book is twice as popular as travel books? _____

22 How many more children like mysteries than animal stories? _____

23 How many more children prefer school stories to travel books? _____ ⬤ 6

Underline the right answer in each line.

24 **Round** £3.70 to the nearest pound: £3 £4 £7 £10 £70

25 **Round** £26.01 to the nearest pound: £20 £25 £26 £27 £30 ⬤ 2

26 £
4.39
− 1.72
_____

27 £
0.27
× 5
_____

⬤ 2

26

Ring the correct answer.

28 When you add together two odd numbers the answer is:

    an odd number   an even number

29 If you add together two even numbers the answer is:

    an odd number   an even number

30 If you add together three even numbers the answer is:

    an odd number   an even number

31 If you add together three odd numbers the answer is:

    an odd number   an even number

    4

32 What is the **sum** of the even numbers between 3 and 7?   _____

33 What is the difference between 7 and 19?   _____

    2

34 How many times can I take £1.25 from £6.25?   _____

    1

Write the correct fraction in each space.

35 Shaded   _____

36 Unshaded   _____

37 Shaded   _____

38 Unshaded   _____

39 Shaded   _____

40 Unshaded   _____

    6

Paper 11

1 Sally left home at 08:52 and arrived at school at 09:01.

How long did it take her to walk to school?   _____

2 If I spent 23p and had 18p left, how much had I at first?   _____ p

3 How many children are there altogether in a school if there are 197 boys and 165 girls?   _____   (3)

Here are four regular pizzas. One whole, one cut in halves, one in thirds and one in sixths.

4 How many $\frac{1}{6}$s make 1 whole?   _____

5 How many $\frac{1}{6}$s make $\frac{1}{3}$?   _____

6 How many $\frac{1}{6}$s make $\frac{1}{2}$?   _____

7 How many $\frac{1}{3}$s make 1 whole?   _____

8 How many $\frac{1}{6}$s make $\frac{2}{3}$?   _____   (5)

9
```
   369
   425
 + 264
 ─────
```

10
```
   204
 ×   8
 ─────
```
(2)

11 How many times can I take 9 from 99?   _____

12 From the **digits** 4, 5 and 6 make a number so that the 5 is the hundred and the 4 is the unit.   _____

13 Write in figures two thousand and twenty.   _____

14 How many times can I take 8 from 56? _____ **4**

15–17 Shade in the **hexagons**.

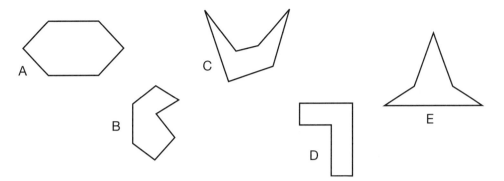

3

18–24 Here are the ingredients for a meal for 1 person.

Jacket Potato with Leeks and Cheese for 1 person	
1 large (about 200 g)	potato
10 g	butter
1 tablespoon	milk
2 (about 150 g)	leeks
40 g	grated cheese

Increase the measurements to change it to a recipe for 4 people.

Jacket Potato with Leeks and Cheese for 4 people	
___ large (about ___ g)	potatoes
___ g	butter
___ tablespoons	milk
___ (about ___ g)	leeks
___ g	grated cheese

7

25–26 18 is half of _____, and three times as much as _____ .

27 How many jars of Bovo, each costing 75p, can I buy with £3.75? _____ **3**

This clock shows the correct time.

How fast or slow are the clocks below?

Write the number of minutes and ring the correct word for each clock.

28–29 _____ minutes   fast

slow

30–31 _____ minutes   fast

slow

32–33 _____ minutes   fast

slow

6

34–38 Each train takes 1 hr 10 min to reach Fordby. Write what time each one arrives.

	Train A	Train B	Train C	Train D	Train E
Leaves Bunmouth at	10:00	11:30	12:50	13:55	15:10
Arrives at Fordby at					

5

Put a sign in each space so that each question will be correct.

39   5 _____ 2 = 2 _____ 1

40   4 _____ 4 = 10 _____ 2

2

Paper 12

1 It is now 2:37 p.m. In half an hour's time it will be _____ : _____ p.m.

2 What time is a quarter of an hour before midnight? _____ : _____ p.m.

3 Six minutes after 10:45 is _____ : _____

3

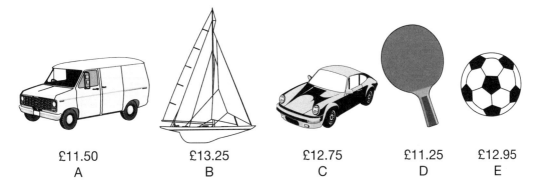

| £11.50 | £13.25 | £12.75 | £11.25 | £12.95 |
| A | B | C | D | E |

4–5 Which two toys could you buy with £23.00? _____ and _____

6 How much would it cost to buy the bat and the football? £_____

7 How much change would you have from £13.00 if you bought a van (A)? £_____

8 How much change would you have from £15.00 if you bought a boat (B)? £_____

9 How much would it cost to buy all the toys? £_____

10 How much would it cost to buy a van and two bats? £_____

7

11–14 Draw the lines of **symmetry** in each of the following shapes.

The first one has been done for you.

4

15–26 The table below should show the important times in the morning at Greenway Primary School.

Each lesson is half an hour long. Break lasts 15 minutes. Lessons begin at 09:30.

Fill in the correct times.

	Begins	**Ends**
First lesson		
Second lesson		
Break		
Third lesson		
Fourth lesson		
Fifth lesson		

12

27–30 Join each three-dimensional object on the left with its **net** on the right by drawing a line.

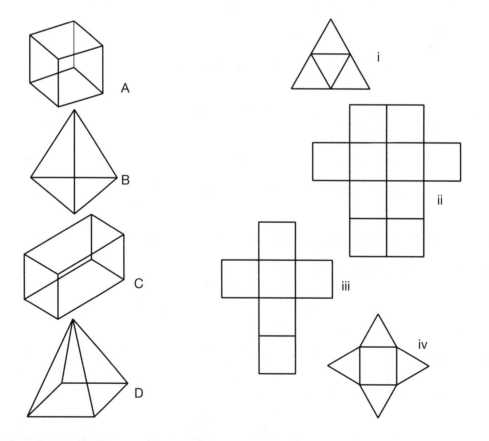

4

31 What is the difference between 1 litre and 850 ml? _____ ml

1

The children in a swimming club made this **pictogram**.

It shows how many children of each age group could swim.

Age 7	🧍 🧍							
Age 8	🧍 🧍 🧍 🧍							
Age 9	🧍 🧍 🧍 🧍 🧍 🧍 🧍 ⸙							
Age 10	🧍 🧍 🧍 🧍 🧍 🧍 🧍 🧍 🧍							
Age 11	🧍 🧍 🧍 🧍 🧍 🧍 🧍 🧍 ⸙							

Key

🧍 = 2 children

⸙ = 1 child

32 How many children in the club can swim? _____

33 How many more 10-year-olds than 8-year-olds can swim? _____

Swimming group A has all the 10-year-olds and 11-year-olds.

Swimming group B has all the younger children.

34 Which is the larger group? _____

35 How many more are in this group? _____

A season ticket for the swimming baths costs £15.00 each.

36 If all the children bought a season ticket, what would
be the total cost? _____

Last Thursday there was a 100 m race. Two of the 9-year-olds entered along
with all the 10- and 11-year-olds.

37 How many were in the race? _____

38 The rest of the children entered the 50 m race.
How many were in this race? _____   7

39 What is the remainder when 28 is divided by 5? _____

40 What is the remainder when 28 is divided by 6? _____   2

Paper 13

Use two of the numbers in the brackets to complete the following **sums**. Do not use the same combination twice.

1–2 _____ + _____ + 9 = 12 (1, 2, 3, 4, 5, 6, 7, 8)

3–4 _____ + _____ + 8 = 12 (1, 2, 3, 4, 5, 6, 7)

5–6 _____ + _____ + 7 = 12 (1, 2, 3, 4, 5, 6)

7–8 _____ + _____ + 7 = 12 (1, 2, 3, 4, 5, 6)

9–10 _____ + _____ + 6 = 12 (1, 2, 3, 4, 5)

11–12 _____ + _____ + 6 = 12 (1, 2, 3, 4, 5)

13–14 _____ + _____ + 5 = 12 (1, 2, 3, 4)

14

15–18 Use the numbers in the brackets below only once to make each side of the square add up to 12. You can use the **sums** above to help you.

(1, 2, 3, 5)

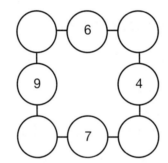

4

19–23 Make these shapes look the same on each side of the **mirror line**.

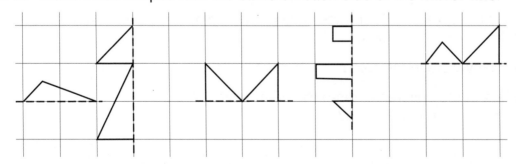

5

Put a sign in each space so that each question will be correct.

24 6 _____ 6 = 4 _____ 3

25 4 _____ 5 = 3 _____ 3

26 6 _____ 2 = 3 _____ 1

34

27 7 _____ 4 = 4 _____ 1

28 8 _____ 2 = 5 _____ 1

29 7 _____ 1 = 4 _____ 4

This bar chart shows how many people got on a bus at each of the four stops in the centre of the town.

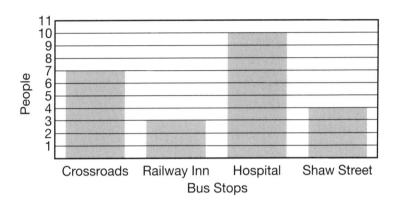

30 How many people got on the bus altogether? _____

31 How many more people got on at the hospital than at the Railway Inn? _____

32 How many more people got on at the crossroads than at Shaw Street? _____

33 How many more people got on at Shaw Street than at the Railway Inn? _____

34 If all the people who got on the bus paid 60p each, how much was this altogether? £ _____

A quarter of the passengers got off the bus at the next stop and 3 more got on.

35 Now how many passengers would be on the bus? _____

Passengers cannot take more than 16 kg on the plane.

36–37 Who was allowed to take all their luggage with them?

_____ and _____

38 Whose luggage is the heaviest?　　　_____

39 How much over 16 kg is his case?　　　_____

40 How much extra weight would Mr Bell be allowed to put in his case to make it up to 16 kg?　　　_____　◯ 5

Now go to the Progress Chart to record your score!　　Total　◯ 40

Paper 14

Write the next two numbers in each line.

1–2	115	110	105	100	_____	_____
3–4	27	31	35	39	_____	_____
5–6	543	538	533	528	_____	_____
7–8	213	219	225	231	_____	_____
9–10	66	77	88	99	_____	_____

◯ 10

11 How many times can I take 7 from 98?　　　_____　◯ 1

Underline the correct answer in each line.

12 12×11　=　112　　121　　123　　132　　144

13 $400 \div 20$ =　40　　20　　200　　400　　4

14 $101 - 89$　=　12　　11　　21　　23　　22

15 $\frac{1}{2}$ hour　=　15 min　20 min　30 min　40 min　45 min

16 70×40　=　280　　2800　　1100　　240　　470

17 $603 \div 3$　=　21　　31　　301　　201　　210　　◯ 6

18 My watch is 9 minutes slow. It shows 5 minutes to 11. What is the right time?　　　_____ : _____

19 When a number is taken away from 21 the answer is 8. What is the number?　　　_____　◯ 2

20
```
   27
   68
   49
 + 36
 ─────
```

21
```
   403
 ×  70
 ─────
```

2

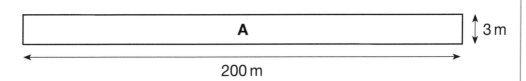

A   3 m

200 m

22 What is the **area** of rectangle A? _____ m²

23 What is the **perimeter** of rectangle A? _____ m

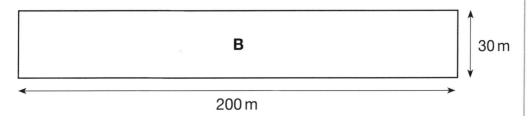

B   30 m

200 m

24 What is the **area** of rectangle B? _____ m²

25 What is the **perimeter** of rectangle B? _____ m

26 How many times bigger is the **area** of rectangle B than the **area** of rectangle A? _____

27 By how much is the **perimeter** of B bigger than the **perimeter** of A? _____

6

28 From the **digits** 7, 8 and 9 make a number so that 9 is the hundred and 8 is the unit. _____

29 What is the **product** of 10 and 100? _____

2

Write the answers to the following questions.

30 $12 \times 8 = 10 \times 8 + 2 \times 8 = $ _____

31 $15 \times 7 = 10 \times 7 + 5 \times 7 = $ _____

32 $18 \times 5 = 10 \times 5 + 8 \times 5 = $ _____

33 $16 \times 9 = 10 \times 9 + 6 \times 9 = $ _____

4

My brother has 40 counters.

18 are yellow, 15 are green and the rest are blue.

34 How many are blue? _____

35 How many times can I take 6 from 72? _____ ◯ 2

To make a rosette you need 15 cm of ribbon.

36 How many could you make with a metre of ribbon? _____

37 How much ribbon would be left over? _____ ◯ 2

38 What is the **sum** of the odd numbers smaller than 10? _____ ◯ 1

39 What needs to be added to change 5864 to 7864? _____

40 What needs to be subtracted to change 6842 to 6342? _____ ◯ 2

Now go to the Progress Chart to record your score!   Total ◯ 40

Paper 15

1–2 Fill in the missing numbers on this number line.

‾22   ‾21   _____   ‾19   _____   ‾17   ‾16   ◯ 2

3 How many weeks are there in 28 days? _____ ◯ 1

Here is part of a centimetre ruler.

4 How far is it from A to B? _____

5 How far is it from D to G? _____

6 How far is it from G to K? _____

7 How far is it from F to H? _____

8 What is the distance between A and C? _____

9 How far is it from A to K? _____

10 How far is it from B to J? _____

11 What is the distance from C to F? _____ ⓐ8

12 The film lasted 153 min, which is _____ min to the nearest 100 min.

13 Oxton to Cowster is 197 miles, which is _____ miles to the nearest 10 miles.

14 The return trip (from Oxton to Cowster and back) is _____ miles to the nearest 10 miles. ⓐ3

A   B   C   D   E

ⓐ3

15–17 Shade in the **quadrilaterals**.

18 What is the **product** of 6 and 21? _____

You start with 16 eggs. Half are broken so you throw them away. Half of the unbroken eggs are too old so you throw them away.

19 You are now left with _____ good eggs.

20 Twice nine is _____ ⓐ3

Our class

Black shoes   11   5   8   Grey socks

3

21 How many children are in the class? _____

22 How many children are wearing grey socks? _____

23 How many are wearing black shoes? _____

24 _____ children are wearing grey socks and black shoes.

25 How many children are not wearing black shoes? _____

26 _____ are not wearing grey socks.

⬤ 6

27 I spend 27p. What change should I receive if I give
the shopkeeper £1.00? _____ p

⬤ 1

The time is 5 to 8. How fast or slow are these clocks?

Write the number of minutes and ring the correct word for each clock

28–29 ____ minutes   fast

                        slow

30–31 ____ minutes   fast

                        slow

32–33 ____ minutes   fast

                        slow

34–35 ____ minutes   fast

                        slow

⬤ 8

36 What needs to be added/subtracted to change 7812 to 7212?

_____

37 What needs to be added/subtracted to change 6324 to 6354?

_____

38 What is the largest number you can make with these **digits**:
2, 5, 8, 6, 5? _____

39 Now write it in words.

_____

40 Write in figures four thousand, one hundred and twenty. _____

⬤ 5

Paper 16

1–3 What fraction of the board is shaded? Underline the correct answers.

$\frac{1}{2}$ $\frac{1}{3}$ $\frac{1}{6}$ $\frac{1}{12}$ $\frac{2}{3}$ $\frac{2}{6}$ $\frac{2}{12}$ $\frac{3}{6}$ $\frac{3}{12}$ $\frac{6}{12}$

4–5 What fraction of the paperclips has been ringed? Underline all the correct answers.

$\frac{1}{2}$ $\frac{1}{3}$ $\frac{1}{4}$ $\frac{1}{6}$ $\frac{2}{3}$ $\frac{2}{4}$ $\frac{2}{6}$ $\frac{3}{4}$ $\frac{3}{6}$

6 Which fraction is larger: $\frac{1}{2}$ or $\frac{1}{4}$?   _____   ◯ **6**

Put a circle round the correct answer.

7 $0.25 =$ $\frac{1}{2}$ $\frac{2}{5}$ $\frac{1}{4}$ $\frac{25}{10}$

8 $0.1 =$ $\frac{1}{2}$ $\frac{1}{1}$ $\frac{1}{10}$ $\frac{1}{100}$ ◯ **2**

9 In a sponsored swim, Kevin's dad says he will pay 50p per length.

Kevin swims 13 lengths, so his dad has to pay   £_____   ◯ **1**

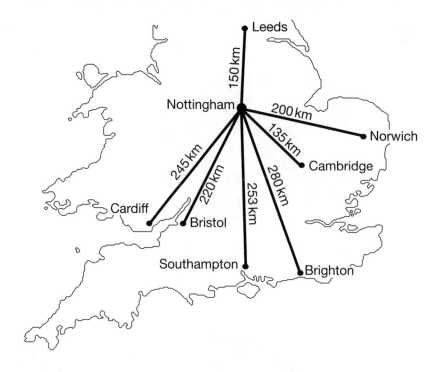

10 Which town is furthest away from Nottingham? _____

11 Which town is nearest to Nottingham? _____

12 Brighton is further away from Nottingham than Southampton is by _____

13 Cardiff is further away from Nottingham than Leeds is by _____

14 What is the distance from Nottingham to Southampton to the nearest 10 km? _____ km

15 What is the distance from Nottingham to Leeds to the nearest 10 km? _____ km **6**

16 Write in figures: eight thousand and eighteen. _____ **1**

17–19 Carefully draw the hands on the clocks on the right so they show the same times as those on the left.

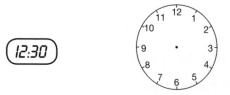

Remember that the hour hand is shorter than the minute hand.

3

20 $\frac{1}{2}$ of 26 = _____

21 $\frac{2}{3}$ of 21 = _____

22 $\frac{3}{4}$ of 16 = _____

3

23 6 paper chains at 80p cost £ _____ .

24 6 strands of tinsel at 85p cost £ _____ .

25 How many Christmas cards, at 45p can I buy with £2.00?   _____

3

Alison weighs 39 kg, Christopher weighs 37.5 kg and Rachel weighs 41.7 kg.

26 Alison and Christopher together weigh   _____ kg

27 How much heavier is Alison than Christopher?   _____ kg

28 Christopher and Rachel together weigh   _____ kg

3

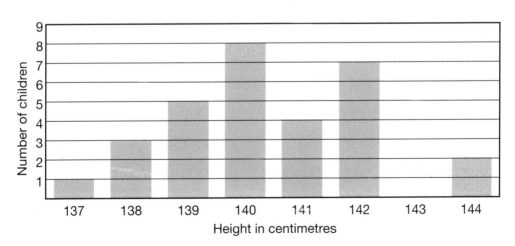

29 How many children are shown on the bar chart?   _____

30 How many children are 143 cm tall? _____

31 How many more children are 140 cm tall than are 138 cm? _____

32 How many children are less than 140 cm tall? _____

33 How many children are more than 140 cm tall? _____ ◯ 5

34 4 m 25 cm + 5 m 75 cm = _____ m

35 8 m 36 cm + 7 m 68 cm = _____ m

36 5 m 0 cm − 2 m 45 cm = _____ m

37 6 m 10 cm − 2 m 70 cm = _____ m ◯ 4

38–39 If 5 m of material costs £6.00, 1 m will cost _____
and 11 m will cost _____. ◯ 2

40 How many $\frac{1}{2}$ hour lessons are there between 09:30 and 12:00? _____ ◯ 1

Now go to the Progress Chart to record your score! Total ◯ 40

Paper 17

Thirty days has September,
April, June and November.
All the rest have 31,
Except February alone
Which has but 28 days clear,
And 29 in each leap year.

1 In June and July together there are _____ days.

2 In March and April together there are _____ days.

3 In February and March together, in a leap year, there are _____ days.

4 When it is not a leap year, how many more days are in
December than February? _____

5 How many years are there in 48 months? _____

6 How many years in a millennium? _____ ◯ 6

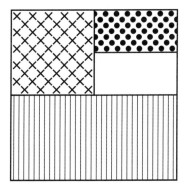

7 What fraction of the picture above is dotted? _____

8 What fraction is striped? _____

9 What fraction is plain? _____

10 What fraction has crosses? _____ 4

11 If three pencils cost 99p what will be the cost of two pencils? _____ p

12 What is the **product** of 7 and 6? _____

13 If 12 books cost £66.00 what is the cost of one book? _____ 3

Put a sign in each space so that each question will be correct.

14–15 7 ___ 1 = 4 ___ 4

16–17 3 ___ 7 = 5 ___ 2

18–19 6 ___ 1 = 8 ___ 1

20–21 6 ___ 4 = 2 ___ 12

22–23 4 ___ 4 = 10 ___ 6

24–25 12 ___ 3 = 8 ___ 2

26–27 2 ___ 7 = 15 ___ 1

28–29 3 ___ 1 = 7 ___ 4   16

30	428	31	3.29	32	3.24
	× 7		× 6		× 7

3

This diagram shows that one whole can be divided into thirds, sixths and twelfths.

1 Whole											
$\frac{1}{3}$				$\frac{1}{3}$				$\frac{1}{3}$			
$\frac{1}{6}$		$\frac{1}{6}$		$\frac{1}{6}$		$\frac{1}{6}$		$\frac{1}{6}$		$\frac{1}{6}$	
$\frac{1}{12}$	$\frac{1}{12}$	$\frac{1}{12}$	$\frac{1}{12}$	$\frac{1}{12}$	$\frac{1}{12}$	$\frac{1}{12}$	$\frac{1}{12}$	$\frac{1}{12}$	$\frac{1}{12}$	$\frac{1}{12}$	$\frac{1}{12}$

33 How many $\frac{1}{3}$s make 1? _____

34 How many $\frac{1}{12}$s make $\frac{2}{3}$? _____

35 How many $\frac{1}{6}$s make $\frac{1}{3}$? _____

36 How many $\frac{1}{12}$s make 1? _____

37 How many $\frac{1}{6}$s make $\frac{2}{3}$? _____

38 How many $\frac{1}{6}$s make 1? _____

39 How many $\frac{1}{12}$s make $\frac{5}{6}$? _____

40 How many $\frac{1}{3}$s make $\frac{8}{12}$? _____   ( ) 8

Now go to the Progress Chart to record your score!   Total ( ) 40

Paper 18

Write the next two numbers in each of the following lines.

1–2	£1.75	£1.50	£1.25	£1.00	_____	_____
3–4	30p	36p	42p	48p	_____	_____
5–6	2015	2025	2035	2045	_____	_____
7–8	$\frac{1}{2}$	1	$1\frac{1}{2}$	2	_____	_____
9–10	1 day	20 hr	16 hr	12 hr	_____	_____
11–12	132	140	148	156	_____	_____

( ) 12

13	22.5 +18.6	**14**	26.5 + 36.5	**15**	38.9 + 43.8

_____   _____   _____

Fill in the missing numbers in each of these questions.

16 $4 \times$ _____ $= 12$

17 $2 + 3 +$ _____ $= 11$

18 $5 \times 6 =$ _____

19 $12 -$ _____ $= 8$

20 $24 +$ _____ $= 30$

21 How many years in 60 months?   _____

Eve bought a book for £4.75 and some writing paper for £1.80.

22 How much did she spend?   £_____

23 How much change would she have from £10.00?   £_____

24 The school hall has 32 rows of chairs and there are 20 chairs in each row. How many chairs are there altogether?   _____

25 What is the **product** of 7 and 12?   _____

26–29 $\times 4$

14	
21	
16	
23	

30–34 $\div 6$

54	
36	
42	
150	
186	

35 How many erasers for 5p each could you buy with £6.85?   _____

36 $50 \times 1 = 60 -$ _____

37 $20 \times 0 = 7 -$ _____

Put the hands on these clocks.

38 25 past 2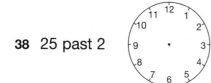

39 $\frac{1}{4}$ to 10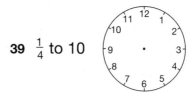

40 10 past 7

○ 3

Now go to the Progress Chart to record your score!   Total ○ 40

Paper 19

1–2 Underline the smallest and circle the largest.

22p,   £2,   £0.02,   £2.22,   £2.02   202p

3–4 Underline the smallest and circle the largest.

623   632   642   640   622   624   ○ 4

5 **Round** to the nearest pound: £9.66 = £ _____

6 Write 964p in £.   964p = £ _____

7 Write metres in centimetres: 34.4 m = _____ cm   ○ 3

8 The age of Bridget, Bob and Sarah add up to 24 years.

If Bob is 8 and Bridget is 7, how old is Sarah?   _____ ○ 1

One side of a **square** room is 6 m.

9 How far is it all round?   _____

10 What is the **area** of the **square** floor?   _____ ○ 2

Here is a timetable for Wednesday morning.

Mathematics	09:15–09:45
Music	09:45–10:30
Break	10:30–10:50
History	10:50–11:25
Games	11:25–12:00

11 We do mathematics for _____ min.

12 Break is _____ min long.

13 We play games for _____ min.

14 We spend _____ min having our music lesson.

15 How long is the history lesson? _____ min.

16 From 09:15 to 12:00 is _____ hour _____ min.

6

17 London to Leeds is 283 miles, which is _____ miles to the nearest 100 miles.

18 The return trip (to Leeds and back) is _____ miles to the nearest 100 miles.

2

19–20 The fuel tank in a truck holds 151 litres, which is _____ litres to the nearest 10 litres and _____ litres to the nearest 100 litres.

2

21 Fill in the missing number in the brackets on this number line.

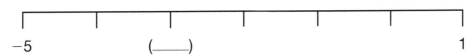

-5   (____)   1

1

22 Put these temperatures in order, lowest first.

5 °C   −14 °C   −1 °C   _____ _____ _____

1

Underline the two questions in each line which give the answer.

23–24	13 =	9 + 3	7 × 2	11 + 2	19 − 6	14 + 1
25–26	$6\frac{1}{2}$ =	$12\frac{1}{2} - 6\frac{1}{2}$	$10 - 3\frac{1}{2}$	4 + 2	$5\frac{1}{4} + 2\frac{1}{4}$	$4\frac{1}{4} + 2\frac{1}{4}$
27–28	5 =	10 − 10	20 × 5	18 − 13	15 − 5	5 × 1

6

29	88		30	709		31	709
	77			× 8			× 80
	+ 66			———			———
	———						

3

Here is a **pictogram** which shows the number of people who had tea at Meg's Café last Thursday.

 represents 5 people having tea.

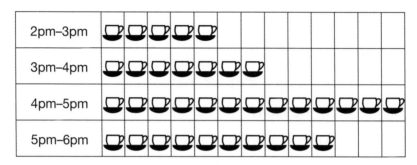

32 How many people had tea at Meg's Café between 2 p.m. and 4 p.m.? _____

33 How many had tea between 4 p.m. and 6 p.m.? _____

34 How many more people had tea between 4 p.m. and 5 p.m., than between 2 p.m. and 3 p.m.? _____

35 If the café charged £4 for a tea how much money was taken last Thursday? _____

Twice the number of people who had tea at Meg's Café on Thursday had tea there on Saturday.

36 How many were there on Saturday? _____

5

Look at this **sum** carefully.

32 + 49 = 81

Now use it to help you with the following questions.

37 81 − 32 = _____   38 132 + 149 = _____

39 181 − 132 = _____   40 532 + 349 = _____

4

Paper 20

Fill in the missing numbers so that each question will be correct.

1	2_	2	40	3	__
	+ 46		− __		× 3
	69		22		105

◯ 3

4 Rakesh gets £2.50 pocket money a week.

  If he saves half of it, how long will it take him to save
  £10.00? _____ weeks

5 How many times can I take 20 from 200? _____

6 A clock is 12 minutes fast. What is the correct time
  when the clock shows 10:25? _____ : _____

◯ 4

7 Find the **sum** of all the even numbers between 1 and 9. _____

8 There are 85 children in Classes 1, 2 and 3. If there are 28 in
  Class 1, and 27 in Class 2, how many are there in Class 3? _____

9 How many are there in Classes 2 and 3 together? _____

10 How many are there in Classes 1 and 2 together? _____

◯ 3

Here are the marks some children got in the last three spelling tests
(out of 10).

	Andrea	Mark	Deborah	Stuart	Alison	Steven
Test 1	7	8	9	7	8	9
Test 2	4	6	8	5	7	6
Test 3	9	10	8	7	9	7
Totals						

11 Who had the highest total marks? _____

12 Who had the lowest total marks? _____

13 Who got fewer than 8 marks in each of the tests? _____

14 Who got 8 or more marks in each of the tests? _____

15 Who got 10 in one test? _____

16 Who had fewer than 5 marks in one test? _____

17–18 _____ and _____ got the same total marks.

Look at the **pictogram** and answer the questions.

Roundabouts	☺☺☺☺☺☺☺☺☺
Scenic Railway	☺☺☺☺☺☺☺☺
Dodgems	☺☺☺☺☺☺☺☺☺☺☺
Swing-boats	☺☺☺☺☺☺
Go Karts	☺☺☺☺

Key

☺ represents
2 people

19 How many more children went on the dodgems than on the swing-boats? _____

20 There were _____ fewer children on the go karts than on the roundabouts.

21 How many children went on the scenic railway? _____

22 What was the total number of children who went on these amusements? _____

4

Maria is 131.5 cm tall. Susan is 3.25 cm shorter than Maria.
Cathy is 4.75 cm taller than Maria.

23 How tall is Susan? _____ cm

24 How tall is Cathy? _____ cm

2

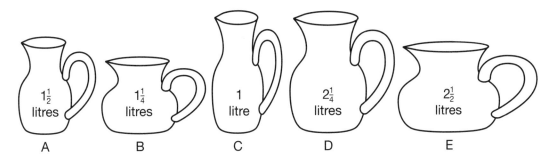

$1\frac{1}{2}$ litres	$1\frac{1}{4}$ litres	1 litre	$2\frac{1}{4}$ litres	$2\frac{1}{2}$ litres
A	B	C	D	E

25–26 Jug _____ holds the most and jug _____ holds the least.

27–28 Jug _____ holds exactly twice as much as jug _____.

29 A beaker holds $\frac{1}{8}$ litre. How many beakers full of water can be poured from jug A? _____

30 What is the total amount that all the jugs will hold? _____ ◯ 6

July					
Sunday		5	12	19	26
Monday		6	13	20	27
Tuesday		7	14	21	28
Wednesday	1	8	15	22	29
Thursday	2	9	16	23	30
Friday	3	10	17	24	31
Saturday	4	11	18	25	

31 If today's date is July 3rd, what will be the date in one week's time? _____

32 What is the date on the third Tuesday in July? _____

33 How many days appear 5 times in this July? _____

34 A fortnight before July 25th is _____ ◯ 4

Fill in the missing numbers in each line.

35–36 $1\frac{1}{2}$ 3 $4\frac{1}{2}$ _____ $7\frac{1}{2}$ 9   _____   12

37–38   115   119   _____   127   _____   135   139

39–40   36   33   30   _____   _____   21   18   ◯ 6

Paper 21

Write these times for the 24-hour clock.

1 5 p.m.   ____ : ____   2 11 p.m.   ____ : ____

3 9:05 p.m.   ____ : ____   4 4:22 p.m.   ____ : ____

5 2:51 p.m.   ____ : ____   6 6:30 p.m.   ____ : ____

7 8:45 a.m.   ____ : ____   8 10:10 a.m.   ____ : ____   8

9 What number needs to go in the box?

2341 = 2000 + 300 + 40 + [   ]   1

10 A ladder is 236 cm long, which is ____ cm to the nearest 10 cm.

11 Two ladders are ____ cm to the nearest 100 cm.   2

12 A chocolate biscuit lasts Amy 55 seconds, which is ____ seconds to the nearest 10 seconds.

13 How long will it take her to eat 4 at the same speed, to the nearest 100 seconds?   ____   2

14 What needs to be added/subtracted to change 8621 to 8221?   ____

15 What number will divide 33 and 44?   ____   2

16–21 Here is part of a tables chart. Complete the empty brackets.

×			
	20	( )	24
	( )	33	( )
	( )	44	48
	50	( )	( )

6

22 How many pence in £14.74?   ____

23 How many pence in £100.30?   ____

24 How many pence in £60.02?   ____

25 How many pence in £0.02?   ____   4

54

26–28 Which of these numbers are exactly **divisible** by 9? Underline them.

15   24   36   46   54   62   72   84   95   98   107

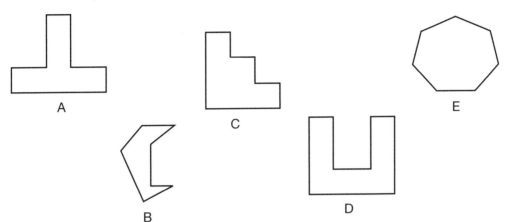

29–31 Colour in any **octagons** below.

A

C

E

B

D

32 Tickets for a concert cost £9.
How many tickets can I buy with £60? _____

Twenty-five children are going to a swimming pool by a minibus which can take 11 passengers.

33 How many trips must the minibus make? _____

34 Write the correct number in the box.

450   ——25 less is——▶   [   ]

35 Draw a circle around the lowest temperature: −7 °C   −9 °C

36 Draw a circle around the lowest temperature: −31 °C   −30 °C

Put a ring round the smallest and underline the largest in each line.

37–38   5412   1452   4251   2415   2514   5214

39–40   8426   4862   6824   8642   6842   4682

Now go to the Progress Chart to record your score!   Total   40

55

Paper 22

Fill in the missing numbers in each line.

1–2   34   28   23   19   ____   14   ____

3–4   ____   9   11   10   12   11   13   ____

5–7 $3\frac{1}{2}$ $7\frac{1}{2}$ ____ $15\frac{1}{2}$ ____ $23\frac{1}{2}$ ____   **7**

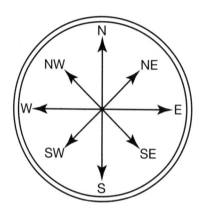

Can you name these compass points?

8 90° clockwise from N is   _____

9 90° anticlockwise from SW is   _____

10 2 right-angles clockwise from S is   _____

11 3 right-angles anticlockwise from SW is   _____

12 2 right-angles anticlockwise from SE is   _____

13 2 right-angles clockwise from NW is   _____   **6**

14 If a goldfish costs £1.25, how many can I buy for £6.25?   _____   **1**

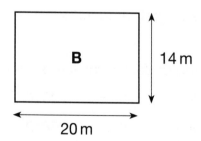

15 What is the **area** of rectangle B? _____ m²

16 What is the **perimeter** of rectangle B? _____ m   **2**

Complete the following lines.

17–18   80   40   20   _____   _____

19–20   12   23   34   _____   _____

21–22   60   80   100   _____   _____

23–24   20   17   14   _____   _____

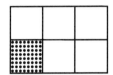

Write the correct fraction in its lowest form in each space.

25 Dotted   _____

26 White   _____

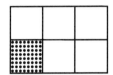

27 Dotted   _____

28 White   _____

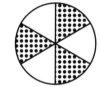

29 Dotted   _____

30 White   _____

31–35 A class of 36 children voted for their favourite school dinners and then made a chart.

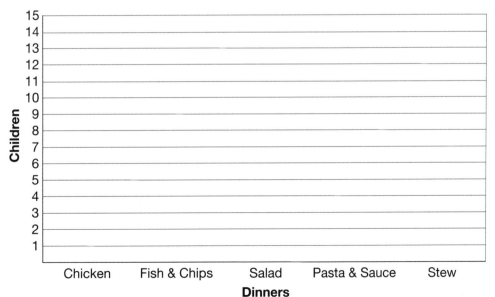

Shade in the columns to show how they voted:

- 3 children voted for salad.
- 3 times as many voted for chicken.
- One third of the class voted for fish and chips.
- The number who voted for stew was one half of the number who voted for fish and chips.
- Both sets of twins in the class, plus two other children, voted for pasta and sauce.

36 The most popular school dinner was _____

37 The least popular school dinner was _____ 7

38 Write in figures nine thousand, two hundred and four. _____

39 Write in figures five thousand and seventy-five. _____

40 The TV programme lasted 138 minutes, which is _____ min to the nearest 10 min. 3

Now go to the Progress Chart to record your score!   Total   40

Paper 23

What number needs to go in the box?

1 $5842 = 5000 + 800 + \boxed{} + 2$

2 $1906 = 1000 + \boxed{} + 0 + 6$

3 $2340 = 2000 + 300 + 40 + \boxed{}$ 3

Write the next two numbers in these lines.

4	8	19	30	41	52	____ ____
5	$4\frac{1}{2}$	7	$9\frac{1}{2}$	12	$14\frac{1}{2}$	____ ____
6	31	27	23	19	15	____ ____
7–8	1	2	3	5	8	____ ____

5

9–15 Complete the following sales board.

SALE	
Ordinary price	Half price
£9.80	
£5.20	
	£2.90
£7.40	
	£2.60
£10.20	
	£4.70

7

Underline the numbers which are divisible by 3.

16–18	69	101	58	405	521	3
19–20	602	73	237	35	852	484

5

Write the name **semicircle**, **equilateral triangle**, **isosceles triangle**, **quadrilateral**, **pentagon**, **hexagon**, **heptagon**, **cube**, **tetrahedron** or **parallelogram** under the correct shapes.

21

_____

22

_____

23

_____

24

_____

25

_____

26

_____

27

_____

28

_____

29

_____

30

_____

31

_____

32

_____

12

33 Which of the shapes on the page before has the most edges? _____

34 James weighs 50 kg, which is ____ kg to the nearest 100 kg.

35–40 Put these numbers in order, largest to smallest.

   3512   2531   3521   1523   2513   1532

  ____   ____   ____   ____   ____   ____

1

1

6

Now go to the Progress Chart to record your score!   Total   40

Paper 24

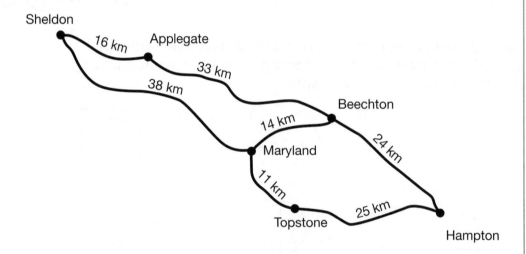

1 From Applegate to Hampton (going through Beechton) is ____ km.

2 From Sheldon to Hampton (going through Maryland and Topstone) is ____ km.

3–4 The shortest journey from Maryland to Applegate goes through _____ and is ____ km long.

5–6 The shortest journey from Beechton to Sheldon goes through _____ and is ____ km long.

6

Look at this calculation carefully and use it to help you with the following questions.

$$27 + 21 \quad = 48$$

7 $\quad 127 + 121 = \underline{\hspace{1cm}}$

8 $\quad 48 - 21 \quad = \underline{\hspace{1cm}}$

9 $\quad 527 + 221 = \underline{\hspace{1cm}}$

10 $\quad 248 - 21 \quad = \underline{\hspace{1cm}}$

Here is another example and set of questions.

$$52 + 16 \quad = 68$$

11 $\quad 252 + 116 = \underline{\hspace{1cm}}$

12 $\quad 852 + 116 = \underline{\hspace{1cm}}$

13 $\quad 68 - 16 \quad = \underline{\hspace{1cm}}$

14 $\quad 768 - 216 = \underline{\hspace{1cm}}$

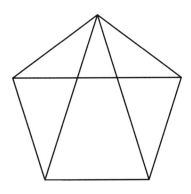

15 What is the name of the outside **polygon**? $\qquad \underline{\hspace{2cm}}$

16 How many **squares** can you find in the polygon? $\qquad \underline{\hspace{1cm}}$

17 What is the name of a polygon with seven sides? $\qquad \underline{\hspace{2cm}}$

Fill in the missing numbers in each line.

18–19	$2\frac{1}{2}$	4	$5\frac{1}{2}$	7	___	___
20–21	33	___	39	42	___	48
22–23	___	38	34	30	26	___
24–25	2p	___	8p	___	14p	17p

Southcross School has 4 half-hour lessons each morning.

26–34 The lessons start at 9:40 and there is a break of 20 minutes after the 2nd lesson. Fill in the timetable.

	Begins	Ends
First lesson	09:40	
Second lesson		
Break		
Third lesson		
Fourth lesson		

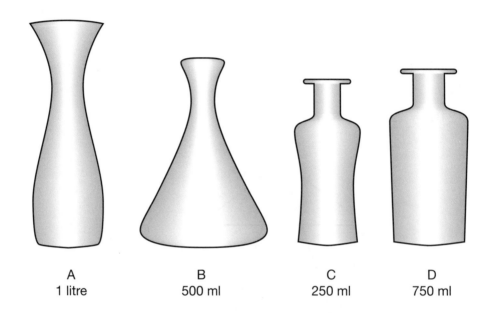

A	B	C	D
1 litre	500 ml	250 ml	750 ml

35 How many times could you fill bottle C from bottle A? _____

36 Bottle A holds twice as much as bottle _____ .

37 Bottle D and bottle _____ together hold as much as A.

38 How much more does A hold than D? _____ ml

39 How many times could you fill C from D? _____

40 468 × 7 = _____

Now go to the Progress Chart to record your score! Total 40

Progress Chart   Maths 8–9 years

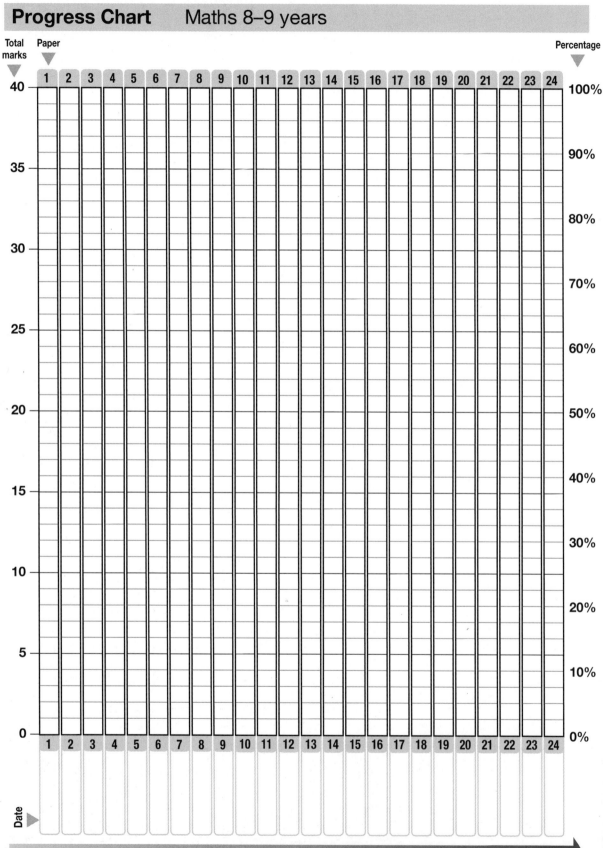

When you've finished the book read the Next Steps

Paper 1

1 5
2 3
3 4
4 5
5 6
6 8
7 14
8 6
9 a square
10 6
11 a rectangle
12 11 min
13 23 min
14 20 min
15 9 min
16 39 min
17 18 min
18 71
19 8
20 82
21 1
22 0
23 2
24 −3
25 −1
26 −7
27 −5
28 −3
29 −1
30 David
31 Daley
32 12
33 12
34 David
35 72
36 120
37 240
38 65
39 85
40 95

Paper 2

1 G
2 F
3 E
4 3
5 1.5
6 11.5
7 14
8 35
9 28
10 42p
11 321
12 312
13 123
14 4000
15 900
16 40
17 4
18 9000
19 600
20 80
21 21
22 27
23 89p
24 21p
25 92
26 35
27 20
28 100
29 £76.00
30 £20.00
31 £6.40
32 £102.40
33 18
34 17
35 6 cm
36 2.5 cm or 25 mm
37 5.5 cm or 55 mm
38 3.5 cm or 35 mm
39 54
40 20

Paper 3

1 9
2 12
3 7
4 6
5 9
6 7
7 25
8 15
9 6
10 9
11 25
12 40
13 45
14 60
15 15
16 seven thousand and one
17 W
18 S
19 NW
20 NE
21 SE
22 S
23 SE
24 60
25 45
26 30
27 16
28 2005
29 2011
30 1999
31–33

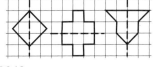

34 8643
35 eight thousand, six hundred and forty-three
36 4320
37 four thousand three hundred and twenty
38 3254
39 15
40 25

Bond Maths Assessment Papers 8–9 years

Paper 4

1 206
2 348
3 £7.40
4 4
5 7
6 12
7 3
8 6
9 23
10 13
11 14
12 3
13 13
14 12
15 26
16 9
17 −1 °C
18 −9 °C
19 2001
20 Martin
21 360
22 Riverside Road
23 Manor Road
24 Farm Lane

25–28

Farm Lane											
High Street											
Birch Avenue											
Riverside Road											
Manor Road											

29 380
30 14
31 92
32 78
33 1
34 2 (Remember, a square is a rectangle with 4 equal sides.)
35 12
36 60 − 5
37 7 × 6
38 299
39 280
40 96

Paper 5

1 −8 °C
2 −2
3 3
4 121
5 5
6 31
7 90 min
8 1500 g
9 102
10 1.5 m
11 21
12 20
13 51
14 40
15 3
16 2
17 3
18 49
19 28
20 56
21 35
22 77
23 36
24 72
25 96
26 24
27 2 cm
28 0.5 cm or 5 mm
29 3.5 cm or 35 mm
30 4 cm
31 4 cm
32 2.5 cm or 25 mm
33 36
34 42
35 35
36 32
37 3 × 22
38 11 × 10
39 10 × 10
40 4 × 40

Paper 6

1 83
2 33
3 108
4 54

5–10

Bus	A	B	C
High Street	2:40	3:50	**4:55**
Broad Lane	**2:50**	4:00	5:05
Market Place	2:55	**4:05**	**5:10**
Kent Road	3:05	**4:15**	**5:20**

11 1.54 m or 154 cm
12 24 cm
13 $\frac{1}{2}$ or $\frac{2}{4}$
14 $\frac{1}{4}$
15 $\frac{1}{4}$
16 twice

17–23

×	4	5	(6)
2	(8)	10	(12)
3	12	(15)	18
4	(16)	20	(24)
5	20	(25)	30

24 656
25 1092
26 +
27 +
28 +
29 +
30 ×
31 +
32 −
33 +
34 25
35 6
36 1
37 20
38 7
39 23
40 6

Paper 7

1 69
2 801
3 963
4 −6
5 −4
6 −2
7 −17 °C
8 −7 °C
9 −4 °C
10 −1 °C
11 0 °C
12 3 °C
13 10:25
14 2 hr 5 min
15 33
16 250
17 60
18 150
19 60
20 2
21 4 × 2
22 3 × 5
23 9 × 4
24 25 ÷ 6
25 4 + 6
26 36 ÷ 3
27 Farway
28 Berrytown
29 180 km
30 4.5
31 8.4
32 745 cm
33 £7
34 8.24 m
35 £3.45
36 B
37 E
38 B
39 D
40 E

Paper 8

1 125
2 29
3 6.5
4 8
5 3
6 7.5
7 7
8 8.5
9 5.5
10 D
11 E
12 250
13 400
14 150
15 250
16 100
17 350
18 4
19 3
20 1
21 7
22 2
23 3
24 2
25 11
26 8
27 5
28 3
29 4
30 9
31 cylinder
32 cube
33 cuboid
34 sphere
35 triangular prism
36 116 cm
37 2400
38 200
39 2640
40 208

Paper 9

1 3
2 4
3 4
4 1
5 (3,4)
6 (4,1)

7–8

9 12.4
10 31.2
11 4
12 15
13 9:42 a.m.
14 33p
15 120 km
16 Monday
17 Tuesday
18 Tuesday
19 Tuesday
20 Friday
21 Sunday
22 3
23 2
24 42
25 Monday 26 Wednesday
27 Thursday 28 Sunday
29 Friday 30 Tuesday
31 D 32 A
33 B 34 C
35 A 36 C
37 D 38 B
39 567, 576, 657, 675, 756, 765
40 198

Paper 10

1 156
2 322
3 5736, 6537, 6573, 7536
4 1
5 4
6 9
7 14
8 3459
9 three thousand four hundred and fifty-nine
10 9543
11 nine thousand five hundred and forty-three
12 15 689
13 fifteen thousand six hundred and eighty-nine
14 98 651
15 ninety eight thousand six hundred and fifty-one
16 1489
17 7089
18 school stories
19 books on hobbies
20 310
21 mysteries
22 10
23 50
24 £4
25 £26
26 £2.67
27 £1.35
28 even
29 even
30 even
31 odd
32 10
33 12
34 5
35 $\frac{1}{4}$
36 $\frac{3}{4}$
37 $\frac{1}{5}$
38 $\frac{4}{5}$
39 $\frac{2}{3}$
40 $\frac{1}{3}$

Paper 11

1 9 min
2 41
3 362
4 6
5 2
6 3
7 3
8 4
9 1058
10 1632
11 11
12 564
13 2020
14 7
15 A
16 C
17 D
18 4
19 800
20 40
21 4
22 8
23 600
24 160
25 36
26 6
27 5
28 5
29 fast
30 10
31 slow
32 20
33 slow
34 11:10
35 12:40
36 14:00
37 15:05
38 16:20
39 − +
40 + −

Paper 12

1 3:07 p.m.
2 11:45 p.m.
3 10:51
4–5 A and D
6 £24.20
7 £1.50
8 £1.75
9 £61.70
10 £34.00
11
12
13
14
15 09:30
16 10:00
17 10:00
18 10:30
19 10:30
20 10:45
21 10:45
22 11:15
23 11:15
24 11:45
25 11:45
26 12:15
27 A − iii
28 B − i
29 C − ii
30 D − iv
31 150 ml
32 62
33 10
34 group A
35 8
36 £930
37 37
38 25
39 3
40 4

Paper 13

1–2 1, 2
3–4 1, 3
5–6 2, 3 or 1, 4
7–8 1, 4 or 2, 3
9–10 1, 5 or 2, 4
11–12 2, 4 or 1, 5
13–14 3, 4
15–18

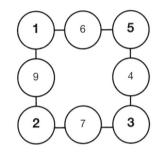

19–23

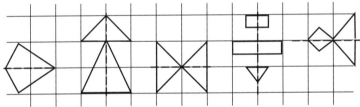

24 + × or ÷ −
25 + ×
26 − + or ÷ ×
27 − −
28 − + or ÷ −
29 + +
30 24
31 7
32 3
33 1
34 £14.40
35 21
36 Mr Bell
37 Mr Eliot
38 Mr Dring
39 5.4 kg
40 7.4 kg

Paper 14

1 95
2 90
3 43
4 47
5 523
6 518
7 237
8 243
9 110
10 121
11 14
12 132
13 20
14 12
15 30 min
16 2800
17 201
18 11:04
19 13
20 180
21 28 210
22 600
23 406
24 6000
25 460
26 10
27 54 m
28 978
29 1000
30 96
31 105
32 90
33 144
34 7
35 12
36 6
37 10 cm or 0.1 m
38 25
39 2000
40 500

Paper 15

1 −20
2 −18
3 4
4 1 cm
5 2 cm
6 3 cm
7 1.5 cm or 15 mm
8 1.5 cm or 15 mm
9 7 cm
10 5 cm
11 2 cm
12 200
13 200
14 390
15 B
16 C
17 E
18 126
19 4
20 18
21 27
22 13
23 16
24 5
25 11
26 14
27 73
28 10
29 fast
30 20
31 slow
32 20
33 fast
34 30
35 slow
36 600
37 30
38 86 552
39 eighty-six thousand five hundred and fifty-two
40 4120

Paper 16

1. $\frac{1}{2}$
2. $\frac{3}{6}$
3. $\frac{6}{12}$
4. $\frac{1}{3}$
5. $\frac{2}{6}$
6. $\frac{1}{2}$
7. $\frac{1}{4}$
8. $\frac{1}{10}$
9. 6.50
10. Brighton
11. Cambridge
12. 27 km
13. 95 km
14. 250 km
15. 150 km
16. 8018

17.

18.

19.

20. 13
21. 14
22. 12
23. 4.80
24. 5.10
25. 4
26. 76.5
27. 1.5
28. 79.2
29. 30
30. 0
31. 5
32. 9
33. 13
34. 10 m
35. 16.04 m
36. 2.55 m
37. 3.40 m
38. £1.20
39. £13.20
40. 5

Paper 17

1. 61
2. 61
3. 60
4. 3
5. 4
6. 1000
7. $\frac{1}{8}$
8. $\frac{1}{2}$
9. $\frac{1}{8}$
10. $\frac{1}{4}$
11. 66
12. 42
13. £5.50
14. +
15. +
16. +
17. ×
18. +
19. −
20. ×
21. ×
22. ×
23. +
24. ÷
25. ÷
26. ×
27. −
28. × or ÷
29. −
30. 2996
31. 19.74
32. 22.68
33. 3
34. 8
35. 2
36. 12
37. 4
38. 6
39. 10
40. 2

Paper 18

1. £0.75 or 75p
2. £0.50 or 50p
3. 54p
4. 60p
5. 2055
6. 2065
7. $2\frac{1}{2}$
8. 3
9. 8 hr
10. 4 hr
11. 164
12. 172
13. 41.1
14. 63
15. 82.7
16. 3
17. 6
18. 30
19. 4
20. 6
21. 5
22. 6.55
23. 3.45
24. 640
25. 84
26. 56
27. 84
28. 64
29. 92
30. 9
31. 6
32. 7
33. 25
34. 31
35. 137
36. 10
37. 7

38.

39.

40.

Paper 19

1. £0.02
2. £2.22
3. 622
4. 642
5. 10
6. 9.64
7. 3440
8. 9
9. 24 m
10. 36 m²
11. 30
12. 20
13. 35
14. 45
15. 35
16. 2 hr 45 min
17. 300
18. 600
19. 150
20. 200
21. −3
22. −14 °C, −1 °C, 5 °C
23. 11 + 2
24. 19 − 6
25. $10 - 3\frac{1}{2}$
26. $4\frac{1}{4} + 2\frac{1}{4}$
27. 18 − 13
28. 5 × 1
29. 231
30. 5672
31. 56 720
32. 60
33. 115
34. 40
35. £700
36. 350
37. 49
38. 281
39. 49
40. 881

Paper 20

1. 3
2. 18
3. 35
4. 8
5. 10
6. 10:13
7. 20
8. 30
9. 57
10. 55
11. Deborah
12. Stuart
13. Stuart
14. Deborah
15. Mark
16. Andrea
17. Mark
18. Alison
19. 10
20. 10
21. 16
22. 76
23. 128.25
24. 136.25
25. E
26. C
27. E
28. B
29. 12
30. $8\frac{1}{2}$ l
31. 10 July
32. 21st
33. 3
34. 11 July
35. 6
36. $10\frac{1}{2}$
37. 123
38. 131
39. 27
40. 24

Paper 21

1. 17:00
2. 23:00
3. 21:05
4. 16:22
5. 14:51
6. 18:30
7. 08:45
8. 10:10
9. 1
10. 240
11. 500
12. 60
13. 200 seconds
14. 400
15. 11

16–21

×	10	11	12
2	20	**(22)**	24
3	**(30)**	33	**(36)**
4	**(40)**	44	48
5	50	**(55)**	**(60)**

22. 1474
23. 10 030
24. 6002
25. 2
26. 36
27. 54
28. 72
29. A
30. C
31. D
32. 6
33. 3
34. 425
35. −9 °C
36. −31 °C
37. 1452
38. 5412
39. 4682
40. 8642

Paper 22

1 16
2 13
3 10
4 12
5 $11\frac{1}{2}$
6 $19\frac{1}{2}$
7 $27\frac{1}{2}$
8 E
9 SE
10 N
11 NW
12 NW
13 SE
14 5
15 280
16 68
17 10
18 5
19 45
20 56
21 120
22 140
23 11
24 8
25 $\frac{1}{6}$
26 $\frac{5}{6}$
27 $\frac{1}{2}$ or $\frac{3}{6}$
28 $\frac{1}{2}$ or $\frac{3}{6}$
29 $\frac{1}{8}$
30 $\frac{7}{8}$

31–35

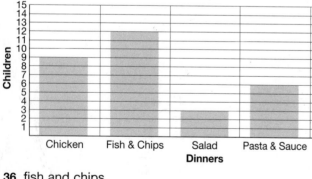

36 fish and chips
37 salad
38 9204
39 5075
40 140

Paper 23

1 40
2 900
3 0
4 63, 74
5 17, $19\frac{1}{2}$
6 11, 7
7 13
8 21
9 £4.90
10 £2.60
11 £5.80
12 £3.70
13 £5.20
14 £5.10
15 £9.40
16 69
17 405
18 3
19 237
20 852
21 equilateral triangle
22 quadrilateral
23 cube
24 isosceles triangle
25 semicircle
26 pentagon
27 tetrahedron
28 hexagon
29 heptagon
30 quadrilateral
31 parallelogram
32 hexagon
33 cube
34 100
35 3521
36 3512
37 2531
38 2513
39 1532
40 1523

Paper 24

1 57
2 74
3 Beechton
4 47
5 Applegate
6 49
7 248
8 27
9 748
10 227
11 368
12 968
13 52
14 552
15 pentagon
16 0
17 heptagon
18 $8\frac{1}{2}$
19 10
20 36
21 45
22 42
23 22
24 5p
25 11p
26 10:10
27 10:10
28 10:40
29 10:40
30 11:00
31 11:00
32 11:30
33 11:30
34 12:00
35 4
36 B
37 C
38 250
39 3
40 3276